LOWESTOFT ANTIQUITY
BY
MALCOLM R. WHITE

Happy Birthday
28.11.02

COASTAL AND MARITIME HERITAGE SERIES

2002

INFORMATION

Published by Malcolm R. White
Coastal Publications
71 Beeching Drive
Lowestoft
NR32 4TB
England, UK

Printed by Micropress Printers Ltd.
27 Norwich Road
Halesworth
Suffolk,
IP19 8BX
England, UK

First Published   November 2002   ISBN 0 9532485 7 7

Copyright © Malcolm R. White 2002   All rights reserved.

Every effort has been made to ensure the information in this book is accurate. For this reason, official documentation, various research works and local records have been consulted for factual support. However, when considering such a complex, variable and historical subject, with some material attributable to other parties, 100% accuracy cannot be guaranteed. As with all other works in this series, measurements, dimensions and distances are stated in British Imperial. Books in this series are part of the National Published Archive, and are included in the library collections of the British Library, the National Library of Scotland, the National Library of Wales, the Universities of Oxford and Cambridge, Trinity College, Dublin, and when appropriate, The National Museum of Science & Industry.

Front Cover

This intricate rail network outside what is now the town centre restaurant of MacDonald's, is similar to that seen today in Manchester and other important towns and centres. However, this is Lowestoft just before the First World War, and the trams were then, as today elsewhere, in much demand. Environmentally friendly tram networks are successfully making a major comeback in towns and cities where there are serious transport and pollution problems. With worsening traffic flow problems in and around Lowestoft, it would be interesting to see what difference modern super trams with their large passenger carrying capacity, speed and comfort could make to the area.

Title Page Photograph

A reminder of a once familiar local maritime scene from the early 1900s. With many sailing trawlers in the Trawl Dock, the tug *Lowestoft* brings a barque into port and through the swing bridge. The tug was built in 1898 at Hull for the then owners of the port, the Great Eastern Railway. After many years service as Lowestoft's most powerful sea going salvage and general towage tug, the *Lowestoft* was broken up at Oulton Broad in 1954.

Opposite Page Photograph

This charming photograph from the late 19th century, shows the view along Claremont Road towards London Road South. Donkeys were very much a part of the seafront and beach scene for at least ninety years. Today this area has been enhanced by very large futuristic black steel hoops incorporating floodlights, which tend to give a tunnel effect to this road, whilst in contrast the adjacent Wellington Gardens have been restored to their former Victorian splendour.

CONTENTS

ACKNOWLEDGEMENTS

Much appreciated has been the support and assistance offered during the preparation of this book by a number of kind and generous people who are interested in researching and recording the heritage and history of the Lowestoft area. In particular, Mr. Stuart Jones BA, who has provided editorial support for all the titles in this popular series, Mr. Jack Cady, Mr. Colin Daines, Mr. Derek Dann, Mr. Peter Killby, Mr. Peter Hansford, Mr. and Mrs. G. Moore, Mrs. Hazel Thompson, Mr. Peter Parker, Mr. David White, Mr. Leo Whisstock, and Louise Clarke and the very helpful staff of the Suffolk Record Office.

PHOTOGRAPHIC OWNERSHIP AND COPYRIGHT

A one time familiar and prominent sign on Horn Hill promoting the well known Lowestoft building firm of Leightons

A scene from the 1870s of a gas lit street which was destined to become part of Lowestoft's main shopping area. Within a few years the trees on the left, part of the Grove Estate, would be felled and development of the area would commence. The fine buildings on the right remain today although somewhat disguised by twenty-first century shop fronts.

A detailed study of a litter and clutter-free Royal Plain shortly after completion in 1903 of the new clubhouse for the Royal Norfolk & Suffolk Yacht Club. In the background can be seen the elegant and very popular South Pier Pavilion, completed in 1891 and demolished in 1954. The fountain seen in the centre of Royal Plain was later moved to Kensington Gardens where it was still working in the 1960s. The Yarmouth "butterfly" pleasure steamer, *Lord Nelson*, can be seen in the Yacht Basin, with the dark sails of a sailing trawler behind her. In the summer of 1904, this vessel and the other "butterfly" vessel, *Lord Roberts,* were running regular trips from Yarmouth to Lowestoft and Southwold.

Introduction

Time moves on at surprising speed, and in the twenty first century, the rate of change appears faster and greater than ever, with Lowestoft continuing to expand and change at an amazing pace. The new visitor, or those returning to the town after an absence of a few years and arriving by road, cannot fail to notice the vast new housing estates built all around the outskirts of the town. At the same time, the once strong diverse industrial heart of the town has been considerably weakened, with a number of major trades, factories and industries disappearing completely. In recent years, the establishment of several new business parks in the town has been seen to be the way forward.

Many of the popular local features, attractions and aspects of the past are no longer with us. However, within the town and the surrounding area vigorous attempts are being made to replace these and entice visitors to the locality by publicising the award winning beach, the attractiveness of the area, promoting the many historic features of the surroundings and offering a diverse programme of special events. These include the annual air festival, an assortment of rallies, fairs, street markets, events and other functions. Many of these are held in the High Street area of north Lowestoft and some on the seafront.

An old Lowestoft guidebook describing the town states, "The town does not rely on the mists of antiquity to attract. On the contrary, it is a progressive resort where nothing is left undone to provide what is now called modern equipment - superbly maintained parks, fine bowling greens, quality tennis courts, immaculate swimming pools, inventive boating lakes, magical concert parties, exciting pleasure steamer outings and an enchanting programme of band concerts all set in numerous splendid and restful locations. These together with the two beaches comprising golden sands, the piers, adjacent Broads, north and south esplanades, and the clean, elegant and charming shopping areas set in the most healthiest environment makes the town the **Queen of Watering Places.** This relaxing resort faces the North Sea to the east and abounds in gentle rolling Suffolk countryside to the north, south and west. The local Suffolk folk are some of the kindest and friendliest to be found and live in a bracing and invigorating climate." At that time, tens of thousands of eager holidaymakers arrived annually, many by direct express trains from various parts of Britain, to stay at boarding establishments, hotels and the newly established nearby holiday camps.

Little was said in past tourism literature about the industrial base of the area apart from the great fishing industry for which Lowestoft was famous and almost every local resident was somehow connected. Whilst in the course of compiling this book, a headline in a local newspaper announced "Another Nail In Town's Coffin". This statement referred to the decision of the very last Lowestoft fishing company to cease fishing operations and the serious financial implications for the town. For many years, the town had the reputation of being one of Britain's premier fishing ports. Fish and fishing, considered by many the reason why a band of hardy folk established a settlement many centuries ago on a spot now known as Lowestoft, has always been a core local industry. However, the industry generally has been in slow decline since the First World War and unless fortunes change or a new company commences operations from the port, the only fish landed at Lowestoft will be by small inshore boats. Other major industries no longer part of the local scene include bus and coach building, railway engineering, motorcar manufacturing, electrical cable and switchgear manufacturing, food processing and canning, boat and shipbuilding, and the manufacture of footwear. These were all sources of substantial investment, prosperity, and long-term employment. They played a vital part in the commercial development and economy of the town. Products made or processed here were at one time found all over the country, and indeed the world.

Another past industry is that of farming, large housing estates and many roads now cover or are planned to cover, vast areas of former farmland between the town and such villages as Oulton and Carlton Colville.

In recent years, many new business initiatives and the allocation of vast amounts of funding from external sources have been announced for the Lowestoft area, and these together with the increasing population could see the area set for a prosperous future and much regeneration.

Our photographic journey commences in the area around the harbour bridge, and then we travel south and clockwise around the town. This book should be considered as a companion to, and complement the sixth book in this heritage series, "Greetings From Lowestoft", which was published in 2001.

Malcolm White
Lowestoft

October 2002

Left - Living in a town divided by an economically important harbour has meant that for generations, getting a "bridger" has been an everyday occurrence. Newcomers or visitors to the area may find being held up by the passage of vessels ranging from small yachts to large container ships through the bridge somewhat frustrating, but for locals it is just part of the normal daily routine. From 1974, this photograph shows a typical queue on the approach to the bridge. Dominating the scene is St. John's Church, which was demolished in 1978. This was designed by John Louth Clemence, and constructed in 1854 by Lucas Bros. Sir Morton Peto contributed towards the cost of building the church, which was one of a number of buildings associated with him in the town, that are no longer to be seen. **Right** - A summer evening study from 1910 of the Inner Harbour. Visible are traders including brigs and barques, ships of the Royal Navy and sailing trawlers.

The second swing bridge at Lowestoft opened in 1897, replacing the earlier one of 1830. In 1969, it suffered a major failure which resulted in the town being effectively split into two parts. This situation was eased by the introduction of a ferry and hastily assembled temporary bridges. Relief came in 1972 with the opening of the present bascule bridge. Portrayed here is the time honoured scene of a local steam herring drifter passing through the bridge. The vessel is *LT534 Go Ahead,* she was built at Colby Bros. Oulton Broad yard in 1919 for the Admiralty as *HMD Volume*. On the 18th November 1940, *Go Ahead* became a total loss following a collision whilst in naval service off Sheerness.

Bridge and Harbour, Lowestoft

"HOME FROM THE NORTH SEA"
A DRIFTER ENTERS LOWESTOFT HARBOUR.
5080

Another familiar feature of the harbour at Lowestoft are the pier head lighthouses. This unusual view clearly illustrates the different styles of the original and the replacement structures. The South Pier lighthouse was rebuilt in the 1930s, but the North Pier lighthouse had to wait until the 1940s for completion of the work. The Consolidated Fisheries steam trawler *LT 84 Croton* is entering port, with the caption on the card indicating that she is a drifter, this is incorrect. Built in 1898 at Govan, *Croton* came to Lowestoft in the 1930s from Grimsby and operated out of the port until 1950 when she was sold for scrapping in Belgium.

Lowestoft was subjected to serious flooding in 1897, with much of the town centre underwater. Belvedere Road was badly affected on the 29th November, when this scene was recorded. Note the boatman going down St. John's Road and the railway truck on the line leading to South Quay. The premises of the building firm Lucas Brothers are in the centre of the photograph. This company was responsible for the construction of many prominent buildings in Lowestoft and elsewhere. Serious flooding, due to high tides and wind, has occurred a number of times in Lowestoft.

LOWESTOFT. THE CHILDREN'S DELIGHT. (105.)

For over one hundred years the antics of Punch & Judy entertained children and adults alike on the seafront at Lowestoft. Presenters of the show during the last fifty years have included Mr. Franklin Spence, Haraldo - Mr. Harold Woolnough and Professor Jingles - Mr. Bryan Clarke. Although this scene is from 1918, it could well be during 1930 or 1990. However, like the show itself, all the fine buildings seen here no longer survive, having been knocked down. For those longing to see Mr. Punch again, he now visits Southwold, where in 2002 he was very busy entertaining large crowds adjacent to the recently restored and popular pier.

Lowestoft certainly knew how to dress up in the 1930s. The South Pier, Bandstand and Pavilion provide a splendid example of grand and elaborate illuminations.

THE PIER AT NIGHT, LOWESTOFT.

G.7849.

Eager to sample the delights of Lowestoft in the summer of 1937, passengers from Great Yarmouth disembark from the pleasure steamer *Lord Roberts* in the Yacht Basin. Sea trips were an important part of many visitors' holidays. Although no longer available at Lowestoft, resorts such as Scarborough, Bridlington and Bournemouth still offer this popular attraction.

Yacht Basin, showing H.M.S. Godetia, Lowestoft

The Royal Navy Fishery Protection Squadron had a long association with Lowestoft, and at one time had a base in the town. For much of that time, when not on patrol protecting Britain's important and substantial fishing interests, their vessels could often be found in the Yacht Basin, available for inspection by the public. Two of the squadron's vessels are seen here in port in 1929.

Lowestoft was a main base for naval operations in the Second World War, initially as *HMS Romola* for use by minesweepers. Later in the war other names allocated to bases in the town were *Pembroke X(Europa), Mantis, Marello, Minos and Minos II(Myloden)*. The harbour became a naval dockyard and scenes such as this, with *MTB 772* in the Waveney Dock, became the norm.
Two armed trawlers can be seen in the background.

Well loved and sadly missed, the miniature railway at Lowestoft operated in two locations in the post war period, initially on the South Pier and later around the now vanished putting green on the seafront. Three different steam locomotives were used on this very popular attraction. Waiting departure with the next train up the South Pier with no doubt a great many happy passengers is *Sonia*. A superbly modelled and valuable engine, the design was based on the well-known London, Midland and Scottish Railway Class 5MT locomotives, the *Black Fives*. It is understood that this engine still exists today in a private collection. Prior to *Sonia*, Lowestoft Corporation owned a small Great Western Railway type steam locomotive and later, an American *Atlantic* type locomotive.

Lowestoft was well known in the 1920s and 1930s for the wide range of quality entertainment the town offered. In addition to the many cinemas, theatres and concert parties, band and orchestral concerts were very popular with the South Pier, in particular, becoming crowded for these performances. An orchestra, appearing at the South Pier, is assembled next to the bandstand for this classic photograph.

Harry Davidson's Commodore Grand Orchestra.

SOUTH BEACH, LOWESTOFT

No, it is not the annual air festival. Despite not having the high tech wizardry of modern aircraft, the town in the past did attract vast crowds to the beach and seafront area, as seen here in the 1930s.

14

Port and harbour related industries such as fishing and the many associated trades, boat and shipbuilding, food processing and marine engineering have traditionally been the mainstay of employment in Lowestoft. Another aspect of the port, which continues to this day, is the handling of general cargo, containers and freight, plus support work for the offshore oil and gas industries, In fact, the harbour was initially built for general trade not fishing. Here we witness a busy scene at the large former Boulton and Paul complex in the late 1950s as three vessels discharge their timber cargos at the quayside.

A great many of the buildings in this 1892 view of the seafront have long been demolished. This terrace of semi detached houses was once a distinct feature of Lowestoft. Another aspect of the seafront we no longer see are deck chairs on the beach and esplanade.

Because of the continually increasing volume of traffic passing through Kirkley, a new stretch of road is planned to enable traffic to bypass that part of the town as it converges on the bridge. There were no thoughts of traffic hold ups in 1896 when this scene was recorded. Today the Hollywood cinema, built in 1927 as the Playhouse, occupies the area in the centre of this view.

Within a company or any business organisation, one of the highlights of the work calendar was the annual dinner or works outing for the staff and employees organised and paid for by the employer. In the post war period, one of the main building contractors in Lowestoft was Leightons. This firm was responsible for the construction of large numbers of houses built locally following the end of the Second World War, and also several prominent buildings. The firm ceased trading in the mid 1950s. Organised by Mr. Reginald Blanchflower, the staff and employees of Leightons are all set for their annual outing in 1948 from their Belvedere Road premises. Some East Anglian companies maintain this tradition thereby creating team spirit and helping to promote good industrial relations. One of the motor coaches being used for the outing, that of the old established Yarmouth firm of Norfolk Motor Services, is seen waiting to depart.

South of the Claremont Pier, construction of the Jubilee Parade was finally completed at the Pakefield end after the Second World War, although work commenced on the project in the mid 1930s. Perhaps this scene from the late 1920s, demonstrates the need for sea defence works. With the sea quite calm and the beach extending to the foot of the cliffs, it is easy to see what damage a high tide and easterly gale could inflict. Unlike today, no effective sea defence groynes are to be seen.

South Beach, Lowestoft

VICTORIA BATHING CHALETS, LOWESTOFT

A short distance further south and close to the spot where on the 2nd August 2002, an RAF Harrier aircraft, serial no. ZD464, crashed into the sea during the annual air festival. By the late 1930s much of the Jubilee Parade was in regular use. Beach and sea shore facilities, familiar at that time, but not today, are illustrated here and include the rafts offshore for swimmers and the boatmen offering family trips on the water in boats with names such as *Dorothy*, *Shamrock* or *Saucy Sally*. In 1936, the Kirkley Hotel, the furthest right of the three buildings on the cliff, advised prospective customers that it offered "irreproachable cuisine".

Now demolished and replaced by a business park, the large cannery owned by the Cooperative Wholesale Society (CWS) makes a fine sight in 1935, decorated for the Silver Jubilee of King George V. This vast factory employed many hundreds of people and this included several members of many families. After closure in late 1997, it was demolished in 2000.

Miss Violet Chipperfield packing portions of cheese spread at the CWS factory in the early 1960s. This was just one of the wide range of food products manufactured there.

Another large cannery to close and located not far from the CWS, was that of Morton's. Originally set up by Charles and Edward Morton, it was part of Beecham Foods from 1955. In the mid 1980s, it was sold to the Hillsdown Group. Both canneries produced a wide range of canned and other food products. Morton's is seen here from the north side of the Inner Harbour. Production ceased in 1988 and demolition of the factory was completed by July 1991.

London Road South appears affluent, clean and tidy on this postcard sent on the 8th September 1920. The premises of Edgar & Co. was one of those damaged on the 25th April 1916 when the German Navy bombarded Lowestoft.

LOWESTOFT. LONDON ROAD, S., (122.)

An early view of the Claremont Pier shortly after the opening in May 1903. The pier has an interesting history with a number of structural changes having taken place over the years.

Sadly today, despite being a focal point of Lowestoft's award winning beach and also the seafront, the seaward end is in an unsafe condition and has been closed to the public for a great many years. This 670 ft. pier was built by the Coast Development Company, one of whose Belle pleasure steamers is seen lying at the pier end. Two bathing machines, a feature of the beach at that time, are in the foreground.

Claremont Pier.   Lowestoft.

No. 1244.

The "Promenade Snaps" taken by Barker's Studio photographers in the area adjacent to the Claremont Pier ensured those happy and relaxing holidays at Lowestoft were remembered. From the 1920s, two ladies are seen walking on the esplanade

In addition to being the main centre for entertainment with every type of attraction which included dance halls, concert parties, bands, variety shows and cinemas, Kirkley's shops catered for every household item that was ever likely to be needed. Apart from the hospital, there was no need to "go over the bridge" for anything. Two of Kirkley's vast range of shops and tradesmen are illustrated here. **Left** - No longer do we see the likes of Mr. Holmes, the shoemaker of Beaconsfield Road, in Lowestoft. **Right** - The staff of the Kirkley branch of the International Stores stand proudly outside their shop in 1914.

The cycle business of J. M. Bird in Kirkley was well known, but as with a number of other small businesses, it is no more. This scene was recorded when British built bikes were still considered the best, and the shop had diversified into selling electrical goods. The property is at present in use as a fast food takeaway. The shop next door was at one time a greengrocers.

An everyday sight for many of the workforce of Richards Shipyard and the food processing factories of Morton's and the Cooperative Wholesale Society, was the very large number of swans to be found in the Inner Harbour. These usually congregated in the vicinity of the outfalls of the food factories. At other times they could be found on the foreshore of Richards shipyard. With the closure of the factories the swans disappeared. A small number of the swans are seen here at Richards in 1978.

23

Left - The number of vehicles on the roads in and around Lowestoft in 1925 was very small, and local residents Mr. and Mrs. Burcham often enjoyed cycle rides from the town centre into the quiet adjacent countryside. They are seen here near Carlton Colville at a location now totally occupied by housing. Mr. Burcham was involved in the installation of the first radio receivers in local fishing vessels. **Right** - Another local scene from 1925 shows a loudspeaker van belonging to the well-known aero, automobile, marine and radio engineering company run by G. F. Surtees from his Bevan Street premises. The much-admired van is parked adjacent to the Royal Hotel. On the wall can be seen an advertisement for "Hard and Grass Tennis Courts on hire for 3/- per hour", another advises customers to book in advance for a grand selection of tours in the "First Class Coaches" of Classic Coaches. A special tour on this day was to Sotterley Woods via Beccles, the fare being 2/-. Other delights advertised are the cruises to Southwold for just 2/-.

Almost everybody in South Lowestoft knew of Hailey's department store in London Road South. In March 1980, this large well liked store suffered a fire which led to its permanent closure and subsequent demolition. A block of flats now stands on the site. This view shows the fire damaged store awaiting a decision to be made upon its future, and with the building in its the final form with the front extension over the pavement. The name of a previous occupier, L. H. Brighton, is clearly displayed.

No longer available for the kiddies and mums and dads to enjoy, the popular seafront boating lake with canoes and paddle boats, was closed and filled in. The adjacent coffee lounge was also closed and later demolished. This prominent location is now part of the large grassed area known as Royal Green which is used for a variety of purposes, such as accommodating travelling fairs and circuses, car boot sales, food villages in connection with the air festival, band contests, car and motorcycle rallies, and pop concerts.

In the 1950s, the Guinness clock soon established itself as a nearby major attraction with crowds watching the fascinating and clever movements, and listening to its magical sounds.

Wellington Gardens occupy a prominent position on the seafront. A restoration scheme carried out in recent years has seen this delightful scene from the early 1930s greatly altered with little of the fine detail seen here remaining today. The imposing 1850s built terrace of houses, part of the original scheme to develop South Lowestoft, was designed by John Thomas.

WELLINGTON GARDENS, LOWESTOFT.

Lowestoft. Kirkley Cliff

Kirkley Cliff is immediately to the south of Wellington Terrace and stands in an outstanding position with superb sea views. Unfortunately, the incline on which the terrace is built, results in additional noise from the large amount of traffic that continually passes this location.

Produced direct from a fine quality glass negative, this print provides a detailed account of a typical summer's day on the Lowestoft south beach in the late 19th century. A great many bathing machines are evident together with the hand capstans used for pulling them out of the water, as is a tented area with stage and seating for a concert party, possibly that of Will Edwards. Not usual these days in Lowestoft is the sight of a Union Flag (commonly known as the Union Jack) being flown. In those days, displaying the national flag on an everyday basis was part of the British culture. The sails of many trawlers can be seen in the Trawl Dock together with smoke coming from the funnel of a vessel, this is probably a paddle tug.

Kensington Gardens, Lowestoft & Pakefield.

L. L Copyright. Lwt. 59.

This was perhaps the most impressive view to be witnessed in South Lowestoft. It is a panoramic view looking south from the top of the tower of the Empire Hotel, later to become St. Luke's Hospital. Recorded in the mid 1920s, just after the Kensington Gardens had opened, the bandstand and general layout of the gardens are quite plainly seen. On the cliff top to the centre left of the photograph is the Grand Hotel with a vast area of gardens and trees to the rear. Only two cyclists are using Kirkley Cliff Road, what is now the main southbound A12 trunk road.

An earlier view from the Empire Hotel, this scene is believed to have been recorded shortly after the hotel opened in 1900. This very rare photograph shows part of the extensive grounds and the land beyond, which would later be used for the creation of Kensington Gardens.

A fine early 1930s view looking north from the top windows of the 1893 built Grand Hotel. Kensington Gardens, opened in 1922, are on the left with the large building of St. Luke's Hospital, completed as the Empire Hotel, dominating the scene. The Jubilee Parade has yet to be built with many people strolling along the beach behind the breakwater.

Lowestoft Corporation Tramways commenced passenger services in July 1903. Here we find tram No. 1 having reached the southern terminus at Pakefield, ready to make the return journey north. G. F. Milnes & Co. built the trams, and double deck cars such as No.1, had seating for a total of 48 passengers. In May 1931, the tramway ceased running and motor buses took over the services.

The electrically driven boats on the boating lake at Kensington Gardens were very popular and remembered with affection by many people. Since this photograph was taken in the mid 1950s much has changed. The many islands have been replaced by one single island and the electric boats replaced with canoes. The aviaries, another long standing popular attraction in the Gardens were dismantled in November 2001, the birds being found new homes. At the time, Council plans were to replace the aviaries with flowerbeds as part of a large scale scheme to refurbish and reorganise Kensington Gardens.

Everyday typical street scenes, recorded many years ago, have an attractiveness of their own. Two Pakefield roads are featured here.

Church Road eighty years ago may look familiar to us today as All Saints Road. The name of the road was changed in the 1930s.

A fine portrayal of the pleasant, quiet and almost rural atmosphere of Florence Road in 1930. The one solitary motorcar tends to look out of place. Maybe it belongs to the Doctor visiting a patient.

With only a cyclist, a carriage, and a tram heading towards the terminus at Pakefield, London Road South in 1909 presents an air of tranquillity. One unchanged aspect of this scene, the entrance to Kirkley Cemetery, is on the right.

The erosion of the cliffs at Pakefield is well documented, but this scene provides a good demonstration of the power of the sea and what it is capable of. A wave crashes into the base of the cliff at Pakefield, with property still standing on the edge above. Brickwork, woodwork and a section of roof can be seen in the water at the foot of the cliff, remains of a building that has already been taken by the sea.

LOWESTOFT. OLD HOUSES. PAKEFIELD. (91.

Pakefield Street was just one of several roads and streets where many properties were lost due to the cliff erosion. Not all were actually destroyed by the sea, many were demolished before the sea took them and the materials from the properties were recovered for reuse.

Left - Within a few years, as the sea continued its relentless drive towards the cliffs, these dwellings at the end of the street would be no more. This scene is from just before the First World War. A well known feature at the end of the road, the red lamp, can be seen near the group who are passing the time away having a "yarn". With all of the buildings in front of these dwellings already gone, marvellous sea views would have been possible from the bedrooms but it is doubtful if the residents appreciated them.

Below - The notice on the boarded up window space may indicate earlier intentions to remain open, but with the building partly dismantled, the Cliff Hotel would never open again. The date is 1907.

The major part of Pakefield was incorporated within the boundary of the Borough of Lowestoft during 1934, by which time a large area of the old village had been lost.

Taken on the morning of the 24th January 1955, this unusual shot of Pakefield shows an approaching snow shower about to envelop the church. On the night of the 21st April 1941 this fine church was burnt out when incendiary bombs, dropped from enemy aircraft, fell on the building. The church was fully restored and on the 29th January 1950 re-dedicated.

Large scale building developments have become common around the town in recent years. Within three miles of the town centre, this rural scene from 1955 is no more. Today it consists of busy roads, bungalows and houses.

Until the new road and the latest bridge were built at Oulton Broad, Bridge Road was the main road through what many refer to as the "village". Two views of the important junction with Victoria Road and Beccles Road, are presented here. Oulton Broad became incorporated in the Borough of Lowestoft in 1919.

A quiet scene from 1905 with no pavements and apparently unmade roads. The properties on the left remain to this day, but many of those on the right no longer exist, being demolished as part of the road improvements of the 1990s.

The Street, Oulton Broad

We move forward in time 27 years, and find the rural atmosphere of the village has been somewhat eroded. With the increasing number of vehicles on the roads, a police officer is seen on duty controlling the now busier junction and the house on the corner of Victoria Road is now a shop. The buildings near what is now the Yacht Station have been demolished.

A steam launch is seen entering the lock which allows passage between the Broad and Lake Lothing in this 1880 view of Oulton Broad. There have been two Wherry Hotels, and the original building of 1859 is in the background.

The second Wherry Hotel had been completed when this scene was recorded before the Great War. A Thames sailing barge and at least three wherries are present at the granary, and a loaded wherry is near the entrance to the lock and the hotel.

A fine postcard published by the well known boatyard and provision stores of Leo Robinson at Oulton Broad. Well before the widespread use of glass fibre in boat construction, all the classic cruisers are built of wood.

BROADSIDE YACHT STATION, OULTON BROAD.

The Boys Brigade and Girl Guides parade through Oulton Broad in 1950. Many changes took place with the building of the new road and bridge in the early 1990s, including demolition of much of the property on the right of the photograph.

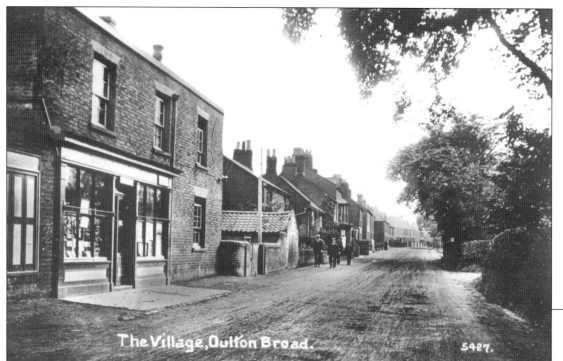

The Village, Oulton Broad. 5427.

Although a great many have disappeared, the Post Office and perhaps the village shop, have always been instrumental in bring the folk of a small community together. In this peaceful scene from the early 1900s, the present Oulton Broad Post Office is on the left. With the greatly increased population of the surrounding area, especially that of the "new" Carlton Colville, this office together with the helpful and pleasant staff is in much demand today.

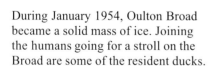

During January 1954, Oulton Broad became a solid mass of ice. Joining the humans going for a stroll on the Broad are some of the resident ducks.

For many years lifeboats of the Royal National Lifeboat Institution visited Fletcher's boat yard at Oulton Broad for refits. The Aldeburgh No. 1 lifeboat is being put back into the water in this mid 1950s scene, following completion of the work. Mr. Peter Parker, well well known in the town as the Chairman of the Lowestoft & East Suffolk Maritime Society, is on the far right of the group.

Lake Lothing has traditionally been of great economic importance to Lowestoft with several important shipyards having been sited on its banks. Many maritime related industries and businesses still trade and operate from premises fronting the lake. This unusual view, from the 1920s, is well before any substantial development had taken place on the south bank.

The high quality work produced by Lowestoft's skilled tradesman went far and wide. This is the scene in the Joiners Shop at the famous Brooke Marine shipyard during the spring of 1956. The shop was located on the upper floor of the north annex to the main east fabrication building at the south shipyard.   Furniture is being made for the twenty large Russian trawlers and other vessels being built at the yard. Brooke Marine ceased trading in May 1987, but the shipyard remained open until 1992 after being purchased by a new company, Brooke Yachts (International) Ltd. In March 1993, tools and equipment previously used for shipbuilding were sold off at auction.

A very proud day for Brooke Marine and Lowestoft. A large group of Brooke Marine employees are seen gathered for the presentation to the Company of the "Queens Award to Industry" on the 9th May 1968. Interesting aspects of this photograph are the clothes, headgear and shoes being worn. In 1968, Brooke Marine had yet to introduce a scheme to supply clothing, protective footwear and headgear to their employees, and the employees themselves provided the items being worn here. The vessel in the background being fitted out is *H.M.S. Fox*, the third of four similar Royal Navy coastal survey ships built at the yard.

A few new churches have been built in Lowestoft in the last fifty years, one of which is St. Benedict's on the corner of Hollingsworth Road and Yarmouth Road. The church is nearing completion in this 1955 view.

One has to look very carefully to identify this section of main road. To many people, it may be totally unrecognisable. The large north Lowestoft Tesco supermarket is now on the fields to the right of the photograph, and a vast housing development now occupies the fields to the left. The photographer would today be standing in the middle of the large busy roundabout with the roads leading to Oulton Broad, Tesco's store, Pleasurewood Hills Theme Park, Great Yarmouth and Lowestoft. The milk churns have been left for collection at the end of the farm drive. The year is 1957.

Over the years the Sparrow's Nest park, together with the now demolished theatre have rightly received great attention. The much loved theatre, in which many great stars appeared, was demolished in 1991. For many people the summer show at "the Nest" was a fundamental part of the Lowestoft holiday season, and of the town. After being used by the Royal Naval Patrol Service (RNPS) during the Second World War, the theatre retained a strong bond with former members of the RNPS. This view, from the early 1930s shows the theatre on the right and café on the left. The building of which the café formed part, was substantially altered during the war years.

The Sparrows Nest, Lowestoft.

Cottages Gun Lane. 19.

Although Gun Lane still exists today, it bears little resemblance to the Gun Lane of the past. The wide scale demolition of properties in north Lowestoft in the late 1950s and early 1960s decided the fate of these dwellings in the Lane. Despite the emphasis that is put on the High Street today as "Historic Lowestoft", the fact is that the great majority of the historic parts of the town no longer exist.

Mr. John Walter Brooke arrived in Lowestoft in 1874 and purchased a small iron and brass foundry in Shuckfords Lane, at the top of Clapham Road. His premises were gradually extended and by the late 19th century were known as "Adrian Works" and situated in Alexandra Road. By 1902, his company was building quality motorcars. All components required for these vehicles were produced on site including the engines. Later the company built small motorboats and established a yard at Oulton Broad. Eventually, the company became Brooke Marine, a major force in British shipbuilding. This view is of Adrian Works in 1926. These works closed in 1938 when production was concentrated at their yard on the banks of Lake Lothing.

Not far from Shuckfords Lane, we would have found these delightful premises. Situated in St. Peter's Street at the top of Arnold Street. They are seen here when in use as shops and dwellings. This building is believed to have been at one time Skoyles Foundry, and the location is now in the middle of the A12 trunk road coming from Yarmouth. The Old Market Plain was at the rear of this building.

Another thoroughfare that exists today although much altered is Dukes Head Street, seen here in the mid 1950s. Within a few years this location would be transformed into a section of main road.

All these buildings in Mariners Street were to disappear in the demolition, during the late 1950s and 1960s, of much of the old and historic parts of Lowestoft. Included amongst these dwellings was reputedly the oldest house in the town, built in the early 1500s and at one time the *Mariner's Inn*. This property is seen on the right of the row of houses.

Mr. Parkes, the optician, and Mr. Gall, the hairdresser, were in business for a great many years from these small shops in St. Peter's Street. Facing the Triangle market place, this photograph was taken when the road was still in use, and before it became a pedestrian area. With the traffic removed, the Triangle has been used for a great many special events including fairs, street markets, art and other exhibitions in recent years.

Lowestoft's main shopping area has seen many changes over the years with several different retailers establishing shops in the town and others leaving. One long established retailer that has been trading in Lowestoft for over 100 years is Morlings, whose shops have been traditionally known as the "House of Music". A branch of Morlings in London Road North is seen here with the neighbouring stores of shoe retailer Freeman Hardy Willis and Craiks, the local confectionary, florist and greengrocery business. The Odeon cinema is just visible. Morlings present Lowestoft premises are at 149/151 London Road North.

At first glance, the High Street appears similar today to this view in the 1890s. However, many changes have taken place since this scene was recorded. The most radical of these was the demolition and consequent setting back of many properties on the west side of the street north from, and including parts of the Town Hall, in the late 19th and early 20th centuries. Many new shop fronts have been introduced, some totally out of character with the surroundings, neon signs are now to be seen and brightly coloured buildings and large modern style painted signs are becoming established.

Left - The *Cosy Corner* was in the High Street at the top of Old Nelson Street and was one of at least eleven cinemas that have existed in the town. Built in 1914 it became the Regent in 1932. After closing and standing derelict for many years, the building was converted into a retail shop. This has had a number of uses including being used for the sale of furniture and soft furnishings and later as a DIY store. Presently it is the Frank Coleby Sportswear Shop. **Right** - With many properties destroyed or damaged following the Second World War, attractive seascapes such as this were possible from Old Nelson Street, London Road North and the High Street for many years in the post war period. Looking across a wartime bombsite, a steam drifter can be seen returning to port from the herring grounds in the early 1950s.

Lowestoft lifeboat station was established in 1801, and for many years the exploits of the RNLI lifeboats were displayed on these boards on the north side of the swing bridge. Passed by thousands of vehicles and people each day, the information boards, together with the photographs, were always a major source of interest for visitors, holidaymakers and townsfolk alike. Today this scene is totally unrecognisable with every aspect having been changed including the demolition of Thains restaurant and the tower of the department store of Tuttles having been destroyed by fire. The date is the 25th August 1961.

Somewhat hidden from view in the busy main shopping area of the town are the offices of solicitors Norton, Peskett and Forward. Many will not realise that the building in this idyllic scene from the mid 1800s, is in fact today part of their offices. At the time this wonderful scene was captured the house was surrounded by open country. Widescale development of the town was someway off, with developer Sir Morton Peto yet to carry out his grand plans south of the harbour.

Almost all those who lived in Lowestoft prior to the building of Katwijk Way will instantly recognise the popular drinking establishment, seen here in 1974. Demolished to make way for the new road, the all white Stone Cottage was at the junction of Bevan Street and Tonning Street. Also in Tonning Street and Bevan Street were premises belonging to the well known electrical retailer Hughes with their notable "TV" sign on the roof. Just visible is a sign pointing the way to the railway station via that handy shortcut, Junction Passage.

Another well-known feature in the town centre was George Armes furniture shop on the corner of The Marina and London Road North. The Marina road at that time ran between two openings in London Road North, and had access from Battery Green by a narrow road adjacent to the Great Grimsby buildings (now the Jobcentre). Here we find the shop in the final days before closure in 1974. The building was destined to become home to a shoe retailers shop.

Often little attention is paid to sights and features we encounter as we go about our daily routine, and on reflection it is often surprising to realise what has changed.

Examples of this are these three retail premises, *Liptons, Mullanes* and *Coles*, which were part of the main shopping centre in the recent past, and have now passed into the history book. The year is 1982.

A number of churches in and around the town have either been converted for other uses or been demolished. The largest of these was St. Peter's which was located at the top of Alexandra and Tennyson Roads. Built in 1832 as a replacement for the small thatched church at one time situated on the site of the Town Hall, and as a Chapel of Ease to the Parish Church of St. Margaret's, it was demolished in 1975. This scene was recorded in 1974, when the building had already been unused for some time.

The bottom of Old Nelson Street was once graced with these fine buildings. This lovely 1893 scene shows the location before Bishops shop was built on the corner of Whapload Road and Old Nelson Street. A major traffic roundabout on the A12 trunk road now occupies this site. The general store seen here, later became owned by G. Nobbs, the shipping supplier.

In the early 19th century, local beachmen formed themselves into "Companies" for the purpose of carrying out life saving and salvage work on the many wrecks offshore. In Lowestoft, there were three such Companies, the Old, Young and North Roads. Each owned sailing yawls and gigs for pilotage work. These brave and stout hearted fellows saved countless lives as well as much valuable property in often stormy conditions. When not at sea the men usually could be found at their "shod" on the beach. The Old Company "shod" is seen here suitably decorated with ships figure heads, names boards etc.

Believed never to have been published before, this primitive 1850 photograph of the early Lowestoft lighthouse proves that many of the published sketches of this structure were somewhat inaccurate. An interesting assortment of buildings on the beach can be seen.

Strand Cottages were situated in the Beach area of north Lowestoft. Here we find some of the residents of these cottages assembled in the street for the photographer. Anguish Street, from where this photograph was taken, ran approximately parallel to East Street and Whapload Road in the area near Christchurch.

Prior to the building of the Britten Centre during the late 1980s, the Eastern Counties Omnibus Company garage was situated at the bus station in Gordon Road. Although the bus station remains at this location, the garage was demolished and new premises acquired close to Ness Point, thereby becoming Britain's most easterly garage. Bristol Lodekkas, a VR and Leyland National buses are seen here in the livery of Eastern Counties, then part of the National Bus Company. Opening in 1919 as the Regent Alfresco, a theatre and concert hall, it closed in 1922 and became a bus garage in 1930s.

In 1974, the Lowestoft Corporation bus undertaking became known as Waveney District Council Trans port, and in late 1977, the undertaking passed to the Eastern Counties Omnibus Company. During the last few months of council run services, a Leyland Titan PD2 double decker of the council fleet, joins London Road from Stradbroke Road in Pakefield. The date is the 14th July 1977.

Lowestoft has had three rail links of which two, to Ipswich and to Norwich, remain. The third, sadly missed today, was to Great Yarmouth. It passed through what are now well-populated areas, and also close to where the District Hospital is situated. Lowestoft Central station was substantially altered in 1992, when the overall roof was removed and the building generally modernised.

Above-Looking across the concourse on the 15th December 1985. The Christmas tree on the right was provided annually by the station staff and was much appreciated by passengers using the station. Usually a collection box for a local charity was situated on or near the tree. Other features not seen today are the station bookstall, roof, chocolate machine, and to the left on the floor, the doggie drinking bowl. A Class 105 diesel multiple unit is in Platform 4.

Right- Looking towards the concourse from Platform 2 on New Years Day 1986, we seen the barriers and the polished buffers and lamp tops for which Lowestoft station became well known.

A carnival procession passes the Central railway station as it heads north up London Road North in 1897 as part of Queen Victoria's Jubilee celebrations. Within a few years, this scene was to change with the coming of the electric tram and the necessary rails, overhead wire support columns, and the electrical supply wires. Crossing the road in the foreground are the railway lines which were last used in 1973 when they carried trucks containing fish offal from the docks.

A quality print from about 1870 showing the original swing bridge of 1830, the first fish market and a barge being loaded, by hand, with coal. In the channel is the paddle tug *Powerful,* she was built in 1856 and first arrived at Lowestoft in December 1858. After working in and around the port for six years, *Powerful* was sent in 1864 to work at Harwich. Unsuccessful there, she returned one year later, and in 1901, was broken up.

Fish Market. Lowestoft. W 2555.

Due to a number of difficulties facing the industry, in August 2002 it was announced that the last Lowestoft trawlers were to be taken out of service and the training scheme for new fishermen ended. When this scene was recorded, the fishing industry had few problems. The Waveney Dock, seen here with many sailing luggers and drifters, was opened on the 1st October 1883 to cope with the seemingly ever increasing demands of the fishing industry. Superb facilities were provided by the Great Eastern Railway, with the large rail served covered herring and mackerel market having full office and fish selling facilities provided for the merchants, buyers and agents, and a broad working area together with good quay headings. Initially this dock was known as the Herring Basin. This view dating from the period around 1890 shows the area before any property existed on Battery Green Road

The parks and gardens tended by the gardeners of Lowestoft Corporation and now Waveney District Council, have long been admired for their delightful layouts, well selected range of colourful plants and well maintained lawns, trees and shrubberies. Even in the immediate post war period in the late 1940s, the Corporation gardeners were hard at work producing such wonderful scenes as this. The impressive building of St. Luke's Hospital, completed in 1900 as the 200-bedroom Empire Hotel and demolished in 1958, provides a backdrop to this fine display in Kensington Gardens.

With the building of the new route for the northbound A12 trunk road through north Lowestoft in the 1970s, all properties on the east side of Clapham Road, many of which were good sound houses, were demolished. In addition, a number of commercial premises were also demolished, of which two are featured here. Within a couple of years of these familiar sights being recorded, both properties had been knocked down. **Left** - Towards the top of Clapham Road we would have found the *Anchor of Hope*, one of the public houses belonging to the Great Yarmouth brewer *Lacons*. **Right** - The Victoria Dairy was run for a great many years by Ada Roe, a well known and liked lady in the town. In 1970, Ada died at the age of 111.

The Lowestoft Cooperative Society had many retail premises, and no doubt the best known were those located at 64 Clapham Road, which catered for most household needs. This giant loaf of bread "with a golden crust", together with the attendants on the cart sitting on sacks containing flour from the Cooperative Wholesale Society, and the well groomed horse, make a superb carnival float and is a great credit to the Lowestoft "Coop". These fine buildings were bombed during the Second World War.

For a number of reasons many of the once numerous places of entertainment such as cinemas and theatres have closed. One exception is the Hippodrome, built in 1904. A building with a long history of providing entertainment, including that of being a theatre, cinema, circus, playhouse and bingo hall, it was to suffer a devastating fire on the 31st January 1999. The original building was burnt out and the few remains quickly demolished. A new Hippodrome has now been built on the site of the original building, which is seen here a few years before the fire.

A once common sight off Lowestoft in the great days when the town was home to busy shipyards. A new vessel, in this case the trawler *Suffolk Mariner,* is off the town undergoing sea trials shortly after completion in 1961 at a local shipyard. She was built for Small & Co., a well-known local company by Richards Ironworks. After a very successful fishing career at Lowestoft, *Suffolk Mariner* was sold and left the port for South Africa in 1983.

A typical Lowestoft scene from the days of steam power, and one much appreciated by many visitors and locals alike. A drifter/trawler heads for the fishing grounds in the late 1940s.

A typical Saturday afternoon in 1973 in London Road North. Since the 1970s many changes have taken place in ownership and appearance of many of the retail premises, and some buildings have been demolished. Two of those no longer with us are the Baptist Church on the right, and on the left, the building almost everybody would like to see today, the superb Odeon cinema and theatre. The main change to this area is that it is now traffic free.

A view from the early 1970s of the South Pier area. Many changes have taken place; new shelters have been built and the Bingo has been relocated. The "Space Tower" mentioned in the next caption is visible.

A comprehensive view of the beach, including Children's Corner, and much of south Lowestoft was available from the "Space Tower" at the entertainment complex built on the South Pier in 1956. The tower was just one of many features of the complex, which replaced the earlier Pavilion built in 1891, and comprised two dance floors, amusements, bars, restaurants and a theatre. The complex was demolished in 1989 and the local headquarters and shop of the Royal National Lifeboat Institution now stand on the site.

PHOTOGRAPHIC INDEX

BACK COVER PHOTOGRAPHS

Top-A rare colour photograph from 1949 of the Esplanade, Children's Corner and the South Pier Pavilion. This pavilion was completed in 1891 and demolished during 1954. Note the missing north pierhead lighthouse; this was being rebuilt at the time.

Bottom Left-The much travelled and superb quality workmanship of local tradesmen is mentioned elsewhere. In September 2002, this Wilts and Dorset Bristol VR bus, built at Lowestoft with Eastern Coach Works bodywork, was on front line duty working the important Weymouth to Salisbury route.

Bottom Right-A small example of the wide variety of retail shops trading in Kirkley in 1981. Since then, all have had new shop fronts, or new owners.